Amy, I love you! You come from a po[...]
so highly qualified that you expect that people are as highly
qualified as you. Others can learn from you about how to
find the right professional. So, they're not going to get
crappy advice. We see bad advice all the time and you have
to clean it up. She helps people, and owners build their
businesses, and grow their businesses in ways that, well,
frankly you may never have thought about. You're so
prolific. You're so detail oriented with what you do.

Ken Krell,
Amazing Digital Events

Amy Herrick is a "ROCKSTAR" ! I absolutely loved
having her as a guest on my podcast as well as on my live
stream. She has so much value to give that having one
conversation isn't enough. I highly recommend Amy as a
guest speaker, you will not be disappointed, but you will be
amazed at her wealth of knowledge. Amy Rose is just
amazing. She's great at what she does. She will help you
build your business correctly with the right foundations.
She will help you ensure that you have the things in place
that you need to have in place.

Laquita Monley,
La Quita's ToolBox
Podcast

I love what you're doing. I told you that when I interviewed you. You have so much knowledge. I love finding people who have just a little bit of a different perspective on things because it makes you think.   I've always kind of been questioning if the crowd's doing it, is it really right? I don't know. Is it a group thing? You've given me a ton of value. I really do appreciate all those courses.

Chris Gunkle ,
Unrivaled Experts

Whatever you got that involves detailed numbers, you will not find, in my estimate, a more thorough, careful, helpful hand. You can't do better.

Artie Vipperla,
Psychic Grandmaster, Energy Healer & Spiritual Guide

Helpful. I really appreciated Amy because it's given me direction and my homework. Thank you!

Dr. Oksana Sawiak,
Sawiak Integrative Wellness Institute

How to Identify a Qualified Advisor

Audio Version Included

Amy Rose Herrick

Profit-Building Specialist

International Best-Selling Author

Herrick, Amy Rose

How to Identify a Qualified Advisor

First edition

Christiansted, US Virgin Islands: Amy Rose Herrick

xvi, 68 pages, 9 inches

Financial Advisors | Insurance Agents | Coach | Counselor | Special Advisor

978-1-960427-09-0

2023939484

332.6

Amy Rose Herrick's books may be purchased in bulk for premiums, groups, educational, business or sales promotional use. For information, please write to: Amy@AmyRoseHerrick.com.

Disclaimer: The information and/or documents contained in this book do not constitute legal or financial advice and should never be used without first consulting with other professionals to determine what may be best for your individual needs. The publisher and the author do not make any guarantee or other promise as to any results that may be obtained from using the

DEDICATION

To my past clients and to my new listening audiences.

It has always been a gift to me when the words and knowledge I share with you changes your life in a positive way and I see it happen with you!

Contents

Introduction

Why do you need a book to tell you what financial professionals do?

There is a mistaken notion that professionals with similar titles do essentially the same thing. Nothing could be further from the truth.

You do not go to an Obstetrician for routine eye care.

You would go to another professional starting with the letter "O," an Optometrist.

We can agree that both have medical training, but their specialties and results of their training and licensing are quite different.

I authored this book for consumers who want an easy reference guide to help them select qualified counsel that can serve you best in your area of financial need.

There is too much confusion on the meaning of many professional titles, and more importantly what those titles represent to the consumer.

You may not be an instant expert on the topic after reading this book. The knowledge gained will enable you to save time and money when you are seeking financial advice from professionals by not wasting your time in establishing the wrong relationship for the wrong reasons.

Here are several common titles and related terms we will cover:

Advisor

Adviser (No, that is not a duplicated misspelled title)

Coach

Counselor

Specialist

Consultant

Agent

Representative

Specialist

Fiduciary

Credentials

Licensing

What about the security and privacy of your information shared?

Your personal information is valuable and marketable data to identity thieves. If you think that identity theft or other theft of your personal data or assets cannot happen to you…read the headlines and you will be shocked at the level of technical sophistication these crime rings have developed.

I give you guidance on the questions to ask when you are interviewing and considering professionals to help you understand what safeguards are in place for your personal data. Did you know that recent statistics tell us that about 60% of businesses quickly fail after a data breach? What is the backup plan to protect your confidential data when a firm fails? Would the answer be: "We have a big, unlocked trash bin out back. The afterhours cleaning staff uses it too for all the offices on this strip."? Do you know how vulnerable your records are right now?

When is the best time to ask about guarantees, refunds, or cancellation policies?

We will cover a lot of learning with a short investment of your time that could make your journey to assembling an effective, coordinated advisory team to manage your financial well-being so much easier and cost effective in the future.

To wrap up what you have learned, you will see some helpful checklists at the back of the book to help guide you in building your dream team of professionals.

Now is the perfect time to get started with chapter one entitled "What is an Advisor, Adviser, Coach, Counselor, Specialist, or Consultant?".

To access your free audio version, please use this link:

https://www.moneywithamyaudiobooks.com/how-to-identify-a-qualified-advisor

CHAPTER 1

"What is an Advisor, Adviser, Coach, Counselor, Specialist, or Consultant?"

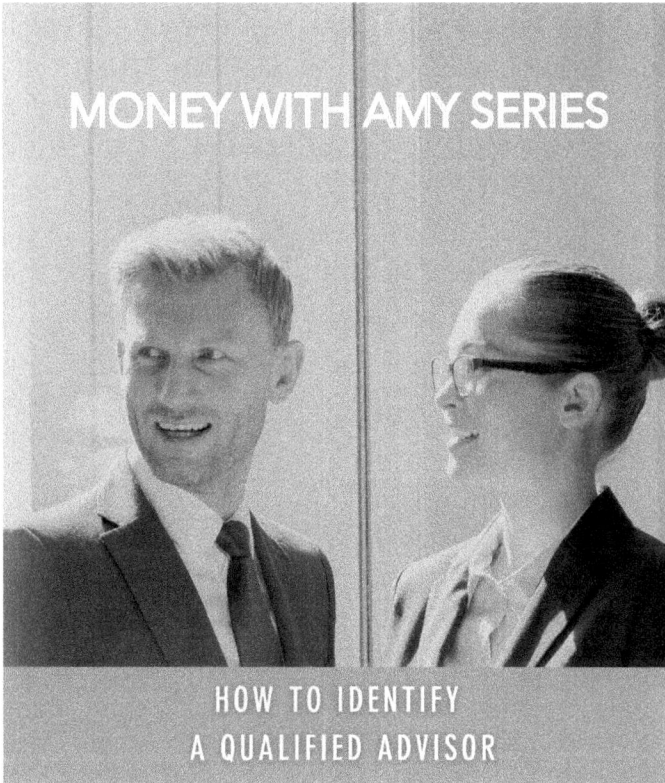

Let us begin with the foundation of the entire discussion.

These phrases are frequently used by professionals to present their titles.

There is no difference in meaning between the spellings "Adviser" and "Advisor."

In many cases, there is no certification that dictates what title is to be used.

Can you discern the difference between these people's offerings, skills, and accessible services? If not, you should inquire about their area of expertise.

- Business Advisor
- Business Adviser
- Business Coach
- Business Counselor
- Business Consultant

What are a few examples or categories of an Advisor, Adviser, Coach, Counselor, Specialist, or Consultant?

You might add these phrases to any of the titles when utilizing any search keyword. I am confident you can generate many more on your own based on your specific requirements and extensively used phrases.

- Business
- Entrepreneur
- Solopreneur
- Financial
- Asset
- Investment
- Income Tax
- Medical
- Legal
- Debt restructuring
- Survival
- Life
- Substance Abuse
- Spiritual
- Grief
- Retirement
- Insurance
- Etc.

What is an agent?

Let us start with an Agent role you are routinely aware of: Insurance Agent.

It is obvious that they work with insurance.

They might be an "Independent Agent." This means they deal with a variety of insurance companies and policy options. They are not contractually bound to only one insurance carrier to give you coverage combinations or rider option possibilities. They have the most product lines available with different insurance companies to meet your needs they can turn to for your circumstances. If more than one company combination is best to meet your coverage needs, they present this option to you.

If they are a "Captive Agent," they are contractually limited to selling just what that one company sells to consumers they are appointed with as an Agent. Coverage options could be limited in this capacity depending on the range and scale of coverage capacity the company has to offer. They may have a narrow specialty market they saturate, or they may offer multiple lines of coverage for a broad presence in different markets.

However, even the title of Agent has specializations in this application. An Agent may have more than one specialist area in which they are trained to assist you.

Property and Casualty Agent

Car   Business
                      Home   Boat
                      Yacht   Etc.

Commercial insurance Agents

Life Insurance Agent

Long-Term Care Insurance Agent

Disability Insurance Agent

Travel Insurance Agent

Group Benefit Agent

Professional Liability Agent

Air Ambulance Coverage Insurance Agent

Heath Insurance Agent

Insurance Brokers

Specialty Insurance Agents:

Some agents specialize in niche insurance areas, such as marine insurance, aviation insurance, or pet insurance, catering to specific client needs.

Even a simple term such as "Insurance Agent" can refer to a variety of expertise and applications for addressing your insurance requirements.

A Representative is someone hired, appointed, contracted, chosen, licensed, approved, or has legal permission to represent a certain company and its products or interests.

The company has the authority to terminate the position of a Representative, usually at any time.

The Representative can give the notice to resign from representing the company, usually in writing, with a specified effective date.

The Representative could act in the best interests of the firm or its product lines within contractual restrictions.

A Representative may do any of the usual roles listed below:

- Accept Orders
- Conduct training
- Collect data for a claim or report
- Serve as a liaison between the client and the company
- Showcase a product
- Etc.

What is the difference between an Emergency Room Doctor and a Specialist?

How does this apply to selecting an Advisor?

The ER doctor never knows what will walk through the door next.

They have been educated to deal with a wide range of medical conditions and treatments. They evaluate the patient, typically with the assistance of other trained professionals, stabilize the patient, and send the patient to other experts to continue care. They do not provide regular follow-up care.

You may simply require one visit for some basic sutures and no referral to another physician.

A specialist has a restricted concentration in their practice on which they focus. They deal with specific pre-set minimal criteria for you to be classified as a potential or eligible patient.

When a specialist is treating many diseases, there may be some overlap.

A pregnant lady may see her eye doctor for glasses and her physical therapist for an ankle injury sustained in a recent fall, but she will not seek obstetrical treatments from either.

They might work together to organize her various care requirements, each specializing in their area.

Are you a business wreck with several issues that need to be addressed, such as cash flow, estate planning, forecasts, inventory control, benefits, and so on? You may not even be aware of all the concerns, but you are aware of a lack of profitability!

In such an instance, you need an Advisor with numerous business analytical abilities, such as an ER doctor, to identify the concerns, treat the conditions that can be treated, and then coordinate with a larger team of specialists, if necessary, when a single visit or professional cannot resolve the multiple issues.

Do you require a specialist in a certain field?

Here is an example of a narrow niche:

> *"I need an experienced grant writer who only works*
>
> *on funding proposals for environmental remediation*
>
> *related to deforestation caused by non-native invasive*
>
> *species to assist me in securing additional funding for*
>
> *a three-year project with my non-profit organization in*
>
> *Washington State."*

There is a difference between what the professionals could or could not do for you based on their skill set or niche experience.

What are you looking for in this relationship?

To illustrate the distinctions even further, let us dive into the necessity of hiring the right specialist for the correct service application. Familiarity with a subject is insufficient.

You should not ask your local Florist to design the titling of your assets or to assist you with your sophisticated estate plan.

Why not?

Just because they sell flowers to many attorneys, banks, and investment firms, and they perform many weddings and funerals for these individuals - acquaintance with them does not make them an expert in these fields or legal matters.

Or do you now seek estate planning assistance from your Florist?

I hope not!

Your florist is not an Estate Planner, Tax Specialist, Lender, or Licensed Insurance Agent!

Why would you want your Florist to do anything other than deliver flower services?

Some of you are doing just that when you contact a bank clerk for tax advice on assets received through an inheritance. Do you understand what the taxation of asset titling entails for your bottom line?

Who do you need to contact for:

- Business Exit Strategies?
- Cash Flow Analysis?
- Business Plan development?
- Staffing Assistance?
- Risk Management?
- Social Media Assistance?
- Investment Advice?
- Debt Management?
- Insurance Coverage?
- Tax Planning?
- Estate Planning?
- Medical Opinions for Treatment Plans?
- Retirement Planning?

Do I need more than one professional on my advisory team?

Yes!

You may have someone who can help you in several interconnected areas, but no seasoned high-quality counsel I can think of does it all alone.

Advisors regularly cooperate with other specialists for the client's benefit in areas where they are not educated, licensed, or trained to best assist you!

How can I benefit the most from my chosen advisor?

Your efforts and how you apply the advice, recommendations, tools, processes, and introductions or opportunities they assist you with to find solutions to your problems will strongly influence your success.

"You can bring a horse to water, but you can't make him drink," as the adage goes.

The identical remark might be rephrased as follows:

"You could advise and show a business owner how to increase profits consistently by making a simple $50 change in their operations that would increase profitability $25k. But I, nor any other advisor, can make them do it."

"You can tell a person to stop increasing debt loads and accruing substantial interest charges by charging expensive meals and vacations they cannot afford on credit cards, they cannot pay off each month while living far beyond their means, but you cannot make them do it."

When you refuse to change your ways or implement solutions or ideas, even the finest Advisor in the world cannot assist you in reaching a new level of success without your engagement and action.

In the following chapter, we will look at credentials, background checks, and other topics.

CHAPTER 2

Why Do Credentials Matter?

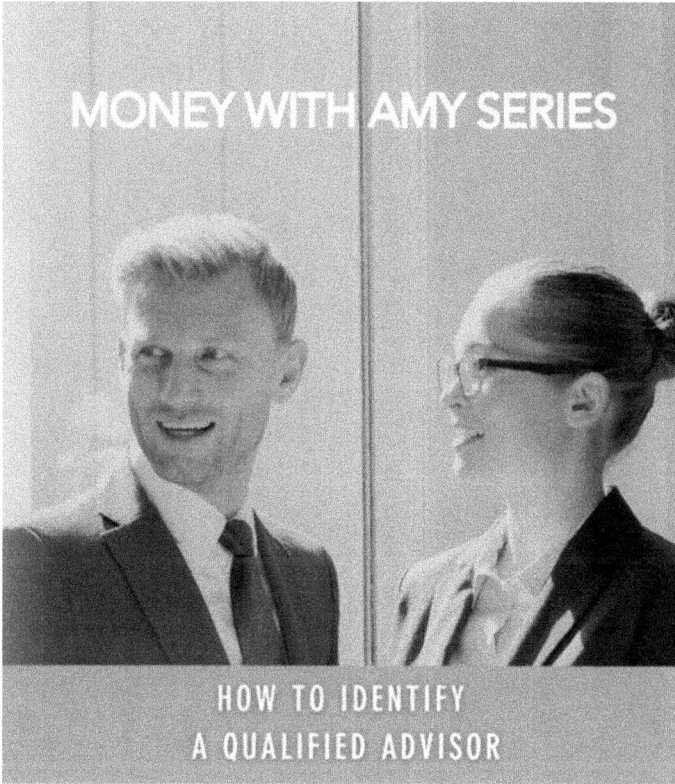

Many credentials require ongoing Continuing Education (CE) credits to maintain the title.

This is to your benefit. When an Advisor stops learning, they soon become obsolete, uninformed, or outdated.

Check to see if the credentials they are claiming are valid.

How?

Inquire as to who provided them with the credentials and verify them for yourself on a matching website or by phone contact.

It is your job to conduct the proper amount of due diligence for the expert you have chosen.

What is a Fiduciary?

An Advisor may be a Fiduciary who is legally bound by specific constraints, or they may be operating as a Fiduciary voluntarily. You must inquire whether this word is applicable.

An adviser may or may not be required to serve as a fiduciary. A fiduciary has a few fundamental responsibilities. They exclusively act in the client's best interests.

For example, if a commission or charge is involved in a transaction, a Fiduciary should offer the solution that best fulfills the client's needs, regardless of how much they would gain from the transaction.

If an outside firm or other resource will better satisfy the client's needs, the Fiduciary should recommend them to that source without hesitation.

A Fiduciary must always manage the property with care and in the best interests of the owner.

A Fiduciary must keep accurate records of all transactions for inspection and tax purposes.

A fiduciary must report to the asset's owner on a regular basis, such as monthly, quarterly, or yearly as agreed.

Disciplinary or complain history should be reviewed.

Conduct a background check! There are several internet services you may utilize to confidentially research public records of your chosen professional under consideration quickly.

It is true, anybody may obtain your or about anyone else's private and professional history for free or by paying a few dollars, and you are not required to be told that your data has been given or sold to anyone.

Perform a web search with the words "complaint" or "scam" after their name. What appears?

A brief check of the Better Business Bureau complaint records may provide some advantages. I do not solely rely on this, but it can provide insight into how concerns were managed in a more public fashion for customers who choose to use this method for resolution of a complaint.

For example, when a licensed professional sells or manages assets such as annuities, stocks, and mutual funds, they should present you with a CRD number if asked for it. You may check here to see whether there have been any disciplinary actions, suspensions, or complaints against these professionals at: https://brokercheck.finra.org/.

You may check with the state Insurance Department to see if an insurance professional's license is in good standing. The Agent may be required to be licensed for multiple insurance lines or several jurisdictions as an agent or non-resident agent.

You may locate a professional with one of my credentials, Chartered Financial Consultant (ChFC), at https://www.youradvisorguide.com/find-a-professional.

Inquire about their qualifications and where you can check they are in good standing. This is not an outrageous request, and they should be able to respond with their identifying data quickly.

What security measures do they have to protect your confidential data?

What information do they need to see or must have to assist you?

How secure are your confidential data or personal information in their systems?

Will the firm you are thinking about sign a non-disclosure agreement if asked to do so?

This is a new development you need to know about. The IRS currently requires professionals working with tax preparation to have a Written Information Security Program (WISP) document.

Have you inquired as to whether your tax preparation professional has created and implemented a WISP as required? Did you know to ask? You do now!

This critical document explains the policies, programs, protocols, and other safeguards that a company or organization has implemented and continues to implement to ensure the security, confidentiality, integrity, and availability of the client's personal information and other sensitive information.

This form of a WISP is intended to encompass the data that the firm develops, gathers, utilizes, and maintains for you.

Every firm should have a WISP to secure sensitive data, whether it is mandated by the IRS, a licensing community, or another organization. It is an excellent business practice to safeguard sensitive data.

This does not imply that the firm must disclose all the facts with you to retain business security. If you ask, they should be prepared to admit or deny having a WISP in writing.

Statistics show that without a WISP, the chances of a firm collapsing within 6 months following a data breach are a frightening 60%.

What would happen to your confidential data in the event of a business collapse caused by a data breach?

If you are a company owner without a WISP, this may be worrisome and disconcerting news for some of you after seeing the closure rates from a security breech above.

You have no idea where to begin or how to set up a WISP.

If you need assistance establishing your own WISP, here is a great resource I can share with you, whether you operate an accounting company or any other type of business: https://tech4accountants.net/amy-herrick/

Do they readily and actively interact with other specialists on/off your current advisor list?

A professional having a network of individuals with whom they can cooperate to suit your needs is more valuable than you know.

They may not only collaborate with your existing Advisors, but they can also serve as a catalyst for strengthening your ties with your pre-selected vendors.

A genuine professional is not necessarily aiming to destroy connections that you have worked hard to build, but rather to strengthen them.

If your Advisor refuses to cooperate with others, they may not be a suitable fit as a collaborator for your personal or commercial goals overall.

Let me give you a tip that will save you a lot of time, money, and heartache: believe your gut sense when it tells you it is time for you to switch to a new specialist. Act on it sooner rather than later.

I would like to take you to the opposite end of the spectrum with a brief graphic.

Even a one-man band can only play a limited number of instruments at once. It is difficult for the individual to excel in all of them at the same time. The performer may be quite good at being loud while also appearing to be terribly busy making different sounds happen, mastering none of the instruments being played.

If your professional refuses to interact with other professionals or never collaborates with them, it may be a clue that working with them long term will be problematic.

They may be unwilling to be questioned or to be offered alternative perspectives to consider.

When questioned, they may be quickly insulted, resorting to the "my way or the highway" impasse that helps no one.

Do they own and manage their own business?

How long have they owned their current business?

How long have they owned other businesses?

What happened to their other businesses?

Sold

Closed

Bankruptcy

Still open

Are they informed about your industry, if applicable?

Do they have any associates? Did you also look at their partner's background?

What would happen to your account and data if they died or were incapacitated unexpectedly tomorrow?

When there is a death or a disability within leadership, is there a leadership transition plan ready to be deployed?

Do they have a buy/sell agreement in place to ensure a seamless ownership transition in the event of a death or long-term disability of an owner?

Do they have a Business Power of Attorney in place for someone to step in if they become ill or incompetent for an extended period?

Do they have an estate plan in place to ensure a seamless succession of the business to heirs or partners if that is the intended outcome?

Have they already worked as W2 employees for another company? In what capacity?

Training and experience levels matter, too!

How long have they worked in this field?

What kinds of advanced training have they received?

Was the training mandatory?

For example, did the individual or the firm they represent pay for the most recent 20 yearly hours of mandatory Continuing Education credits to retain a designation or licensing?

Was the additional education freely obtained?

This additional voluntary training can demonstrate initiative to improve your Advisor's skill set and knowledge base that will be to your advantage.

I consider it added value when professionals use personal resources including their free time to routinely pay for additional voluntary training out of their own pocket.

Why?

This shows me they are willing to invest in their future and put forth extra effort even when it is not convenient or easy without being required to do so.

In the following chapter, we will look at interaction impressions, refunds, assurances, and other topics.

CHAPTER 3

What is your Impression of an Introductory Call?

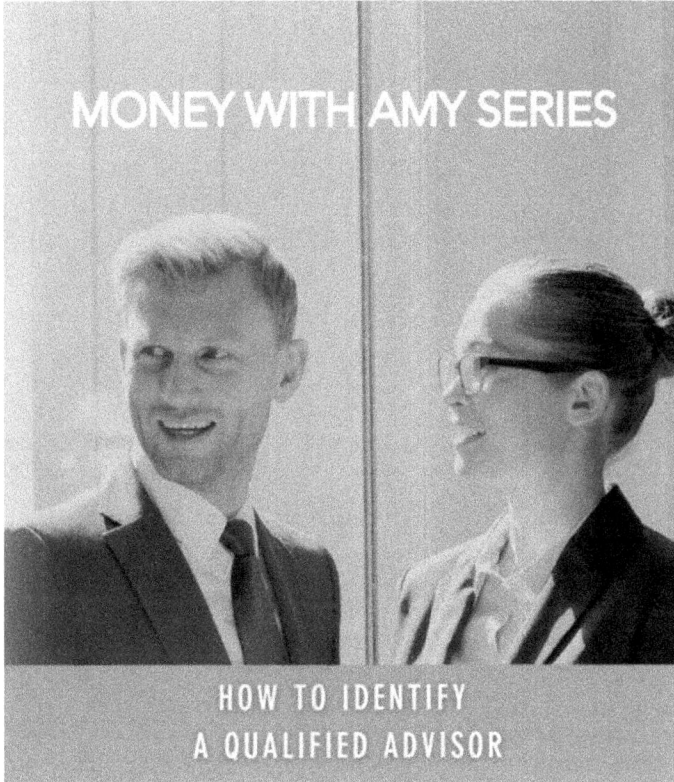

MONEY WITH AMY SERIES

HOW TO IDENTIFY
A QUALIFIED ADVISOR

Do you believe you were heard, listened to, and understood throughout the conversation?

Did you receive anything of value from the chat that you can use now?

Was the expert able to react to your queries without reading from a script and without extended pauses?

Did you leave the conversation wishing for more time with this person or resources that were important to you?

Do you get a "pitched" feeling?

Did you feel pressured to buy now before the price rises?

Did you feel like you needed a bath after being slimed like the character in the iconic scene from the classic Ghostbusters film?

The clarity in services & skills offered

Can you express what they must give you?

Is pricing or a list of services available on their website?

Do you see an opportunity to begin with a basic package and progress to greater levels of service as your company grows?

Do they sell individual components or package services?

Is it possible to evaluate free materials or only paid ones?

Professionals do not work for free!

There are limitations to free information.

Free does not imply inferiority. It is a beginning point for educating the public about what the individual or company has to offer.

In many situations, before the event even began, extremely important material was disregarded as useless by many potential participants, unfairly because the presenter is attempting to assist you to become acquainted by not charging you for attendance.

These specialists spend considerable time and money to give the information to you, your association, or your business at no cost to attend, in exchange for as little as a thank you or a free dinner.

Although you did not pay for it, there was a cost and time commitment in getting the free information to you. The speaker paid for it one way or the other.

A free educational experience is only informative if it is not disguised as a "sales pitch" for a certain product or notion that they want you to purchase.

This is a precious gift of their time and resources, both of which are in short supply for all of us when it is instructive.

Talented professionals cannot and should not volunteer instead of working for free on a regular basis. Do you expect to get paid when you go to work? Professionals in any trade feel the same way.

Do they bill per hour, whether in advance or at the end of the project?

Do they provide services by invoicing a fixed charge in advance or at the conclusion of a project with a list of included items?

Do they provide quantity discounts, prepayment discounts, or bundled services to potentially lower long-term engagement costs for their services?

Many experts are worth 10 times what they charge, and they should be compensated for the value they bring to the table. Too many undervalued professionals need to hike the prices to reflect their true worth! If you are that professional, I give you permission to charge what you are worth if you need it.

Do you purchase online courses that you may access at your leisure?

Are there specific times for sessions that must be scheduled? Will you be able to see a recording of a session if you miss one?

What is their refund, cancellation, or guarantee policy?

What are the conditions for receiving a refund? Is it possible to get a partial refund?

Who pays for shipping on a return if it demands it?

Based on deadlines, how long in advance can you cancel, order, and obtain a 0-100% refund?

How long does it take to process a refund once it has been granted?

For instance, are there specific times for group training sessions that must be scheduled? Will you be able to see a recording of a session if you miss one? For how long will the recording be accessible?

Will your subscription or access to the program be revoked if you miss three sessions of a ten-part series?

Will you be unable to "graduate" if you miss a certain number of sessions, assignments, or deadlines?

Some programs include attendance and study for you to get the most out of your training.

If you cannot regularly attend, the presenter may not want to constantly bring you up to speed.

There may be no reimbursements if you fail to attend sessions that you promised to attend in advance.

If you look at your schedule today, should you postpone your commitment to the upcoming sessions if you notice it will be difficult for you to honor attendance at all meetings?

"Life...HAPPENS!

Not in the way you expect it to happen, but life happens anyway," I frequently remark. "How you react to what happens next is up to you."

In the following chapter, we will investigate testimonials, response times, and referral sources.

CHAPTER 4

Testimonials are not always the Be-All & End-All

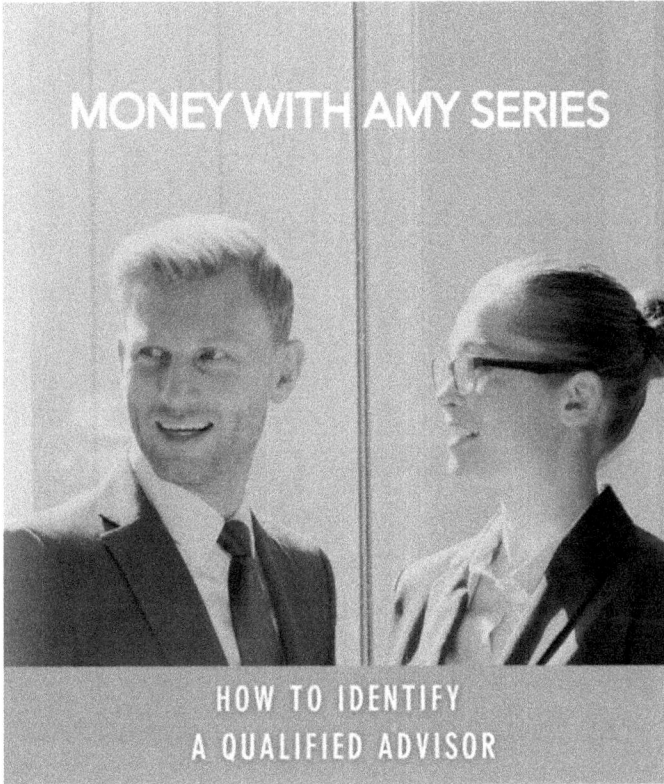

MONEY WITH AMY SERIES

HOW TO IDENTIFY
A QUALIFIED ADVISOR

Look for interviews, podcast appearances, media quotations, articles, books, and appearances on YouTube channels, etc. that will allow you to hear or observe this individual in action in an unscripted manner.

Can they think on their feet and deliver meaningful replies to each interview question?

Is there anything on their search page?

Do they just have one tale or point of view that they repeat over and over?

Testimonials are important to have since people want to see "Social Proof." However, not everyone knew to accumulate testimonials over time to have them ready to go for you to find today. Talented professionals may not have previously populated testimonials on social media or search engines and are playing catchup now.

If you were taught that licensing restrictions limit self-promotion (Yes, it is true that self-promotion constraint is genuine in many professions.), having testimonials may not be something you sought out or have available now. Many great professionals. I know, we are only now learning the rules and catching up on the social media playing field.

Let me return to another point of view here: how often do you read headlines and see reporters wanting to run a story or compile a three-part feature on a person or firm that did an outstanding job on something? A common answer I get when asking that question: rarely or never.

Headlines are often reserved for unpleasant circumstances, crises, conflict, and controversy.

Let me give you a hint, go back far enough and money is involved in some way.

A lack of pages and pages of Social Media Accounts or "Social Proof" may or may not tell the entire story about the quality of the person or firm with whom you are working.

The professional may not be devoting their time and resources to those publicly accessible social media channels to reach their target audience or retain client connections in a more physically based business-building model.

A social media presence is a component of the total due diligence research you may choose to conduct.

How quickly do they respond to new requests?

If you contact us using any agreed-upon channel, such as email, Facebook, messenger, phone, Facebook, WhatsApp, and so on:

How long does it take to obtain a non-canned response?

Let us tell the truth here, we all despise those cheesy scripted automated answers that neither address your query nor connect you to a live human!

Similarly, unless it is an absolute necessity, do not send the same message to all the alternatives. It simply confuses and clogs up the response stream.

Referral Sources

Has your referral source had any personal experience with them? They may or may not be suffering from the same challenges that you are.

Will the referring source get compensated for sending you there, or if you purchase products or services? If this aspect of the referral purpose is significant to you, it is a valid query.

You should be aware that referral or affiliate fees are widespread in many sectors and are utilized to expand a business with like-minded experts.

These business connections are built based on aiding each other with pre-screened recommendations that they trust, and they only send clients who they believe can benefit from what the other expert has to offer. It can, at least, start a conversation between the parties and spare everyone from wasting time and effort looking for help in the wrong direction.

Why are they sending you to this individual? Did you request the referral?

Did you get a cold call from someone saying Bob suggested we meet? If they do not initiate contact or want to be recommended, some potential clients are immediately distrustful or insulted by this surprise business-related gesture.

In the following chapter, we will discuss why you might need a second or third opinion.

CHAPTER 5

Do you Need a Second or Third Opinion?

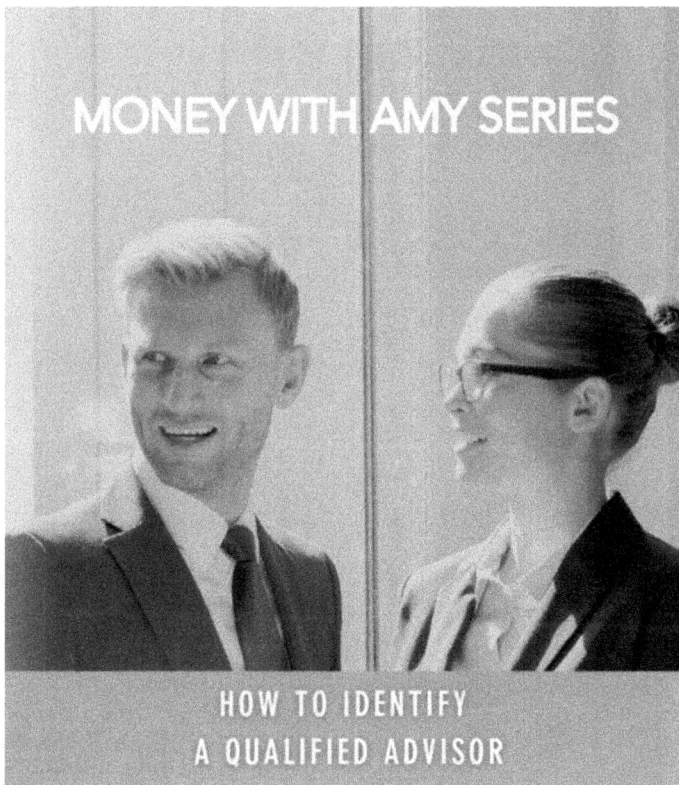

MONEY WITH AMY SERIES

HOW TO IDENTIFY
A QUALIFIED ADVISOR

Some complex circumstances call for a second or third viewpoint.

Many people - I have discovered - will not hesitate to seek a second, third, or even fourth opinion on a significant sickness or surgical operation, but they will hesitate to get even a second opinion on their financial or business concerns.

Inaction can result in a loss of time and money, as well as a detrimental influence on the outcomes you could have obtained if you had acted in a timely and confident manner.

Do you share the same information with potential advisors?

Let me give you an example of how getting a second or third opinion might help you.

You engaged an expert who offered you their assessment of the problem and recommended 10 measures to follow to remedy it, along with the expected outcome, estimated cost, and benefit or gain of each option.

You have never heard of three of these possibilities before, and it will take a significant amount of time and money for you to commit to executing these recommendations. You have no experience whether this is the proper thing to do.

You seek advice from professional number two. You provide them with the same information as professional number one. You provide them with the information they require to make their own suggestions.

Under no circumstances should you share the outcomes of professional number one's proposals to professional number two. Allow them to make their own list and utilize their own resources to develop a plan of action for your review.

It is all too simple to ride on the coattails of others or pick apart their efforts. Show me your own work and let me be the judge of what you have provided.

You go over professional number two's recommendations. If all 10 items they recommend match the list supplied by professional number one, you select the professional you believe is the greatest fit.

But wait, what if professional number two has now presented you with three further unique alternatives that you have never seen before? You are feeling a bit perplexed and wondering if you really understand all your alternatives. Perhaps your position is more complicated than you imagined.

You guessed it; professional number three is hired. You provide them with information. You do not discuss the findings of experts one and two with professional three and then wait for the outcomes.

By this point, you should be well informed about your options and prospective plans of action, and you may have chosen that combining two specialists to complement each other in a joint meeting is the best way to address your complex demands.

Yes, it took longer than you expected in the beginning.

Yes, you may have spent more time and money on the conclusion than you anticipated in a situation where two or three views are required.

I consider this as a wise investment in getting the greatest outcomes for your circumstance, and it will never be money wasted when compared to the expense of the incorrect results from a lack of preparation or proper due diligence that I have seen while attempting to clear up a mess.

Eventually, you will have to live with the consequences of what you did or did not do.

On that topic, I frequently refer to and implement the following quote:

Twenty years from now, you will be more disappointed by the things that you didn't do than by the ones you did do.

So, throw off the bowlines. Sail away from the safe harbor. Catch the trade winds in your sails. Explore. Dream. Discover.

Mark Twain

EPILOGUE

Will you choose a more qualified advisor now?

I certainly hope so!

If not, please contact me and tell me how I can enhance this short resource.

Would you like to schedule a meeting with me to discuss how I can help you increase your bottom line?

Schedule a 15-minute "Amy, make me more money!" phone call here:

https://calendly.com/amyroseherrick/15min

I would appreciate it if you could send me a brief comment with your best takeaway from the resource in your hand as well:

Amy@AmyRoseHerrick.com

CHECKLIST

__Identify what problem you are facing
__Identify what kind of advisor you need help from
__Check your advisor's credentials
__Do a basic background check
__Does your advisor keep your data secured (WISP)?
__Have they owned and/or operated a business?
__How long has the advisor been in the industry?
__Do they have a referral network?
__Do they have licensing or credentials?
__Clarify services and skills offered by the advisor.

__Clarify the payment terms, refund, cancellation, or guarantee policy.

__Look for interviews, appearances, books, quotes, articles, YouTube videos, testimonials, etc.

__Get an opinion
__Get a second opinion if needed
__Get a third opinion if needed
__ Other _____
__ Other _____
__ Other _____

WHO IS ON MY TEAM NOW?

___ Banker

___ Insurance – Car

___ Insurance – Home

___ Insurance – Life

___ Insurance – Disability

___ Insurance – Other

___ Investment Advice

___ Legal Advice – Personal

___ Legal Advice – Business

___ Income Taxes – Personal

___ Income Taxes – Business

___ Debt Structuring

___ Career Advice

___ Higher Educational Resources

___ Other _____

___ Other _____

___ Other _____

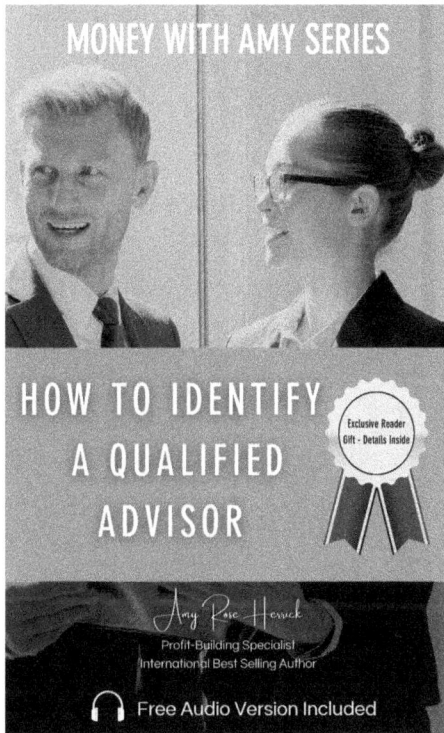

THANK YOU FOR READING MY BOOK!

As a thank-you, we'd love to send you a free bonus book—not for sale anywhere else. Just email us at INFO@AmyRoseHerrick.com with "Bonus Book Request" in the subject line. You'll receive your exclusive gift directly by email.

Loved the book? We'd be grateful for your honest review on Amazon— but the bonus is yours either way.

ACKNOWLEDGMENTS

Without the support of many over the years, I could not be the person I am today. I know I will forget to thank someone, but it was not my intention to do so.

To my family, who do not always understand me, but love me anyway, you mean the world to me.

To friends and colleagues who support my professional talents and literary dreams, I wish you continued success in your endeavors.

To my talented VA team who helped me to have the finished content in print form, may your dreams come true too.

To the online writing groups from around the world on Zoom meetings where we encouraged each other in the manuscript writing processes, I did it and so can you!

To my clients and live audiences who helped me learn so much about this topic with the sharing of their life stories of successes and failures for me to give guidance to you today, thank you for allowing me to have a positive impact on your lives.

To my mentors, I promise to pay it forward.

To my draft version reviewers with all the helpful suggestions and encouragement to get this finished quickly, you will see many of your suggestions incorporated.

And finally, to all the ones behind the scenes we take for granted that make websites, online ordering, eBooks, printing, shipping, and delivery possible for us all…a heartfelt thank you for being a part of my world every day.

About the Author

Amy Rose Herrick, ChFC, is an extraordinary author and financial expert dedicated to transforming lives while empowering individuals and businesses to achieve unparalleled financial success.

Some remarkable solutions take 15 minutes or less to understand and implement.

Her expertise shines brightest creating personalized, comprehensive plans that streamline costs, provide peace of mind, and secure wealth for future generations.

Bid farewell to financial stress while embracing your legacy that will endure the test of time.

Amy, your personal wealth building guide, unleashes the power within your resources.

Complex resource management problems are transformed into easy step by step solutions.

Using groundbreaking methodology, Amy empowers individuals, business owners, and families alike.

Entrepreneurs flock to Amy for clear, actionable tutorials on building more profitable businesses. Under her guidance, ventures can thrive like never before, unlocking their true potential for financial success.

As a fiduciary, Chartered Financial Consultant, and tax professional, Amy has mastered the art of optimizing resources.

Yet, her achievements do not stop there. She is a #1 Best Selling Author, captivating speaker, talented artist, and a dedicated force in community service.

With over three decades of experience, including more than 25 years in the Securities industry, Amy possesses an impressive array of qualifications and expertise. She equips you with the tools to experience lasting financial freedom, providing a transformative journey unlike any other.

In 2023, be prepared for the launch of a series of game-changing books and captivating YouTube videos titled "Money With Amy."

Her dynamic and easy-to-understand content will empower you to strategically structure your resources for the benefit of your family and businesses.

Amy Rose Herrick's list of remarkable accomplishments is truly awe-inspiring. From being named Small Business of the Year to being a #1 Best Selling Author, a National Geographic 'Chasing Genius' Finalist, and even teaching a gorilla named Max, Amy's impact is undeniable.

Clients can expect an unforgettable, life-changing experience with

Amy Rose Herrick, one that simply cannot be replicated elsewhere.

Currently residing by the sea in the breathtaking US Virgin Islands, Amy continues to live a life of abundance while sharing her wealth of knowledge with the world.

Additional Information & Resources

Visit Amy's website: **www.AmyRoseHerrick.com**

Email: **Amy@AmyRoseHerrick.com**

Book a 15-minute Zoom based discovery call to discuss becoming a client for comprehensive financial planning or business profit building assistance at:

https://calendly.com/amyroseherrick/15min

Follow Amy on Facebook

https://www.facebook.com/AmyRoseHerrickProfitBuildingSpecialist

Listen to several Podcast appearances on a variety of topics:

https://www.listennotes.com/search/?q=amy%20rose%20herrick&sort_by_date=0&scope=episode&offset=0&language=Any%20language&len_min=0

Read Amy's articles on Medium at :
https://medium.com/search?q=amy+rose+herrick

Reach out to Amy at Amy@AmyRoseHerrick.com to inquire about booking Amy to be on your show as a guest or for autographed copies.

Watch one of Amy's full length financial literacy building educational videos on YouTube

https://www.youtube.com/@amyprofitspecialist

Linked in: https://www.linkedin.com/in/amyroseherrick/

Instagram: amyroseherrick

Alignable: https://www.alignable.com/christiansted-vi/amy-rose-herrick-chfc-americas-profit-building-specialist

Amazon all current titles for sale link:

https://www.amazon.com/s?k=amy+rose+herrick&crid=SGL1PHGTWZS5&sprefix=amy+rose+herrick%2Caps%2C179&ref=nb_sb_noss_1

Other titles available now, or coming soon, in the **MONEY WITH AMY SERIES** that may be of interest to you:

MONEY WITH AMY SERIES

Building your
foundation:
ENTREPRENEURIAL
MISTAKES TO AVOID

Exclusive Reader
Gift - Details Inside

Amy Rose Herrick

Profit-Building Specialist
International Best Selling Author

Free Audio Version Included

MONEY WITH AMY SERIES

KNOWING YOUR
LIFE PARTNER:

Exclusive Reader
Gift - Details Inside

25 QUESTIONS
TO ASK AND ANSWER
(FOR COUPLES IN THEIR FIRST
LONG TERM RELATIONSHIP)

Amy Rose Herrick

Profit-Building Specialist
International Best Selling Author

Free Audio Version Included

MONEY WITH AMY SERIES

REMARRIAGE:
25 QUESTIONS TO ASK
AND ANSWER
BEFORE REMARRIAGE

Exclusive Reader Gift - Details Inside

Amy Rose Herrick

Profit-Building Specialist
International Best Selling Author

Free Audio Version Included

MONEY WITH AMY SERIES

MARRIAGE AFTER RETIREMENT:

Exclusive Reader
Gift - Details Inside

25 QUESTIONS TO ASK
AND ANSWER
BEFORE YOU MARRY

Amy Rose Herrick

Profit-Building Specialist
International Best Selling Author

🎧 Free Audio Version Included

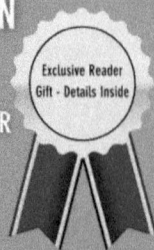

MONEY WITH AMY SERIES

KNOWING YOUR LESBIAN
LIFE PARTNER:
25 QUESTIONS TO ASK AND ANSWER
FOR LESBIAN COUPLES
IN THEIR FIRST
LONG TERM RELATIONSHIP

Exclusive Reader
Gift - Details Inside

Amy Rose Herrick

Profit-Building Specialist
International Best Selling Author

🎧 Free Audio Version Included

MONEY WITH AMY SERIES

LESBIAN REMARRIAGE:
25 QUESTIONS TO ASK AND
ANSWER FOR LESBIAN
COUPLES BEFORE REMARRIAGE

Exclusive Reader
Gift - Details Inside

Amy Rose Herrick
Profit-Building Specialist
International Best Selling Author

Free Audio Version Included

MONEY WITH AMY SERIES

LESBIAN MARRIAGE
AFTER RETIREMENT:
25 QUESTIONS FOR LESBIAN
COUPLES TO ASK AND ANSWER
BEFORE YOU MARRY

Exclusive Reader
Gift - Details Inside

Amy Rose Herrick

Profit-Building Specialist
International Best Selling Author

Free Audio Version Included

MONEY WITH AMY SERIES

KNOWING YOUR GAY
LIFE PARTNER:

Exclusive Reader
Gift - Details Inside

25 QUESTIONS TO ASK AND ANSWER
FOR GAY COUPLES IN THEIR FIRST
LONG TERM RELATIONSHIP

Amy Rose Herrick

Profit-Building Specialist
International Best Selling Author

Free Audio Version Included

MONEY WITH AMY SERIES

GAY REMARRIAGE:
25 QUESTIONS TO ASK
AND ANSWER FOR GAY
COUPLES BEFORE
REMARRIAGE

Exclusive Reader
Gift - Details Inside

Amy Rose Herrick

Profit-Building Specialist
International Best Selling Author

Free Audio Version Included

MONEY WITH AMY SERIES

GAY MARRIAGE
AFTER RETIREMENT:
25 QUESTIONS FOR GAY
COUPLES TO ASK AND
ANSWER BEFORE YOU MARRY

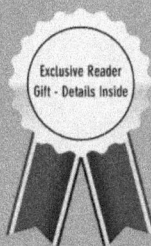

Exclusive Reader
Gift - Details Inside

Amy Rose Herrick

Profit-Building Specialist
International Best Selling Author

Free Audio Version Included

www.ingramcontent.com/pod-product-compliance
Lightning Source LLC
Chambersburg PA
CBHW071504210326
41597CB00018B/2685